The Sockeye Special:
the story of the Steveston tram and early Lulu Island

Best Wishes

Ron Hyde
2012

The Sockeye Special:
the story of the Steveston tram and early Lulu Island

by
Ron Hyde

Richmond, British Columbia, Canada
2011

Copyright © 2011
Ron Hyde

All rights reserved. No part of this book may be reproduced, stored in a retrieval system or transmitted, in any form or by any means, electronic, mechanical, photocopying, recording, or otherwise, without prior written consent of the author.

Library and Archives Canada Cataloguing in Publication

Hyde, Ron
      The Sockeye Special : the story of the Steveston tram and early Lulu Island / Ron Hyde.

Includes bibliographical references.
ISBN 978-1-55383-303-1

     1. Street-railroads--Social aspects--British Columbia--Lulu Island--History--20th century. 2. Street-railroads--Economic aspects--British Columbia--Lulu Island--History--20th century. 3. Street-railroads--British Columbia--Lulu Island--History--20th century. 4. Lulu Island (B.C.)--Social life and customs--20th century. I. British Columbia Historical Federation II. Title.

HE4508.B7H93 2011   388.4'60971133   C2011-906368-9

Cover design by Friesens Corporation
Front cover image: The Sockeye Special car No. 1220, City of Richmond Archives, Photograph #1220.Steveston

Book design by Andrea Lister

Ron Hyde
Box 36513 Seafair PO
Richmond, BC, Canada, V7C 5M4

Printed and bound in Canada by
Friesens Corporation
History Book Division
Altona, Manioba R0G 0B0
Canada

Preface

A message from the author

The research and writing of the *Sockeye Special* and its part in the development of early Lulu Island has been an exciting and rewarding undertaking.

The *Sockeye Special* was an integral part of the transportation, business and social life of Lulu Island.

The story of the tram and its part in the Island's history, gave me the opportunity to present glimpses into Lulu Island's exciting past. For example, the *Sockeye Special* brought thousands of visitors from Vancouver, New Westminster and Richmond to the thrilling horse races at Minoru Racetrack. The tram also brought thousands of visitors to witness several aviation history making events at this track.

Throughout the story of the *Sockeye Special*, you will read historical vignettes and come to appreciate the important impact the tram played in the island's history.

Photographs, research materials, private collections, historical moments, stories and vignettes were graciously shared with the writer and I appreciate the interest, excitement and assistance from so many new and long-time friends.

Special thanks to Bill Purver, Archivist and Dan Farrell and Jamie Sandford of the City of Richmond Archives, Ron Schuss, Vic Sharman, Tony Miletich, Henry Ewert and Bill McNulty. The *Sockeye Special* has been a partnership between the Richmond Heritage Railroad Society and the author.

About the author

Ron Hyde has lived in Richmond since 1958 where he and his wife raised five children.

Ron has been a very active in the community. He is a Charter and Life member of the Kinsmen Club of Richmond, has served on the Board of the London Heritage Farm Society for 21 years, was on the Board for Tourism Richmond for nine years and has been a Board member of the Richmond Museum Society for five years.

During his membership with the Richmond Kinsmen Club, Ron's interest in writing began as Co-Editor of the Club's newsletter, that twice won the provincial newsletter trophy, won the national newsletter trophy twice and was also the runner up in the World Council competition of seventy-three countries.

Ron was a columnist and reporter for the Richmond Scene newspaper where he wrote feature articles on the official opening of the new Vancouver International Airport and the new Canadian Standards Association facilities in Richmond. He also covered the opening of Canada's first McDonald's restaurant located in Richmond and received an award for the grand opening full page advertisement he designed for the paper.

During his 23 years working for the Liquor Distribution Branch (previously the Liquor Control Board) he became their unofficial historian, accumulating historical items, papers and stories of the L.C.B.'s history back to 1921. As a result, Ron set up a small museum in their head office to display this material. Ron also wrote a regular historical column in the L.D.B.'s newsletter *The Grapvine*.

Ron has served on the Board of the British Columbia Historical Federation since 2001 and also was Honorary President for four years. In June 2003, Ron began to write and publish the BCHF quarterly Newsletter.

Ron published a 24 page pictorial booklet with 117 unpublished and little known historical photographs for the Federation in recognition of 150 years of British Columbia's exciting history.

Ron is an active member on the Federation's Publications Committee and also serves as Membership Chair.

Contents

Chapter I	The Beginning of the Transportation System to Lulu Island	1
Chapter II	The BC Electric Railway Co.	11
Chapter III	Other Transportation Endeavors	19
Chapter IV	The Development of Lulu Island and its Community	21
Chapter V	Off to the Races	29
Chapter VI	Social and Entertainment	37
Chapter VII	The Sockeye Special Family	43
Chapter VIII	The Sockeye Special and the Dairy Industry	51
Chapter IX	Rails to Rubber: The Ongoing Demise of the Streetcars and Trams in Greater Vancouver	57
Chapter X	The Richmond Heritage Railroad Society	67
	References	75
	Index	79

Chapter I

The Beginning of the Transportation System to Lulu Island

At the turn of the twentieth century, Billy Steves first threaded his famous stage coach through the tall timbers from Steveston to Vancouver. The trip took a full day. This was the time when Steveston was a thriving seaport, supporting 29 canneries. Ships from around the world moored at the docks to load salmon.

Billy Steves drove his teams over rough corduroy roads. Devotion to his passengers and the Royal Mail, cost him his life one stormy December night when a giant tree crashed across what is now Granville at 37th Avenue — he was killed instantly.

Billy Steves mail and passenger coach
City of Vancouver Archives, Image Str P276

CPR railway bridge over north arm of the Fraser River
City of Richmond Archives, Cars on bridge

In 1891, the Vancouver & Lulu Island Railway was incorporated. The Canadian Pacific Railway (CPR) purchased this railway on August 31, 1901 when they realized there was money to be made by connecting Vancouver with the busy fishing community at Steveston. The Company built a railway bridge with a swing span across the north arm of the Fraser River, just west of the present Oak Street Bridge. Thirty hard working men laid eight miles of track in twenty-two days.

CPR train to Steveston
City of Richmond Archives, Photograph #1977.2.38

The single track stretched across the peat bogs of the fifteen miles long and five miles wide unnamed island. Lulu Sweet, an actress with a traveling theatrical group from San Francisco, became a beloved favourite of audiences during her brief stay. One of her most ardent admirers, was head engineer Colonel Richard Moody, who accompanied the young actress on her departure voyage from New Westminster to Victoria. As the two stood on deck, gazing at passing landmarks, Miss Sweet inquired as to the name of one large island. After replying that the island, as yet, had no name, Moody suddenly exclaimed, "By Jove, I'll name it after you!" And thus, Lulu Island was no longer unnamed.

Lulu Sweet
City of Richmond Archives, Photograph #RCF 21

The original freight and passenger operation was established to service the canneries and their workers, thus the morning and evening schedule. Since Steveston was the only official depot, if others wanted to board the train, they would stand on the track and wave it down. The Sockeye Limited travelled to Steveston pretty much at the speed decided on by the engineer and the conductor, taking into consideration the time to dump off bales of hay and sacks of flour for the logging camps in the Point Grey area. The train consisted of a freight/baggage car and a first class passenger coach with red mohair seats.

The CPR Steveston station was a substantial two-storey 23 foot by 46 foot building located just north of Moncton Street. The station included a ticket and telegraph office, baggage room, general waiting room, kitchen, living room and two bedrooms to house the station master and his family. It also had a 198 foot platform, 510 foot siding and a 30 foot by 60 foot freight shed.

Note: The CPR Station burnt down and was permanently closed May 19, 1929.

The schedule showed two trains daily each way between Vancouver and Steveston, a distance of 16.9 miles. Leaving

CPR Steveston Station
City of Richmond Archives, Photograph #11978.21.28

Eburne Station
Marpole Historical Society collection

the old terminal, the train backed down to Carrall Street, cut across town to the first stop at Hastings Street and proceeded to Granville by the Kitsilano Bridge. The one hour trip from Vancouver included five stops: Magee, Eburne, and three on Lulu Island before arriving at the Steveston terminal.

On June 30, 1902, the CPR had a trial run to Steveston in preparation for the official opening day on July 1st Dominion Day with two trains per day between Vancouver and Steveston.

The $1.50 return trip to Steveston was a popular Sunday afternoon outing for families and couples to enjoy a glimpse of the Vancouver forests and the Lulu Island farm lands.

According to the Steveston correspondent for the *Daily Colonist* noted in article on July 2, 1902:

> *The official opening of the line took place under somewhat inauspicious climatic conditions, but the more important feature of the start, successful running and a well patronized train were all that could be desired.*

Moncton Street, Steveston, circa 1910
City of Richmond Archives, Photograph #1978.37.18

At the Steveston terminal, nearly five hundred passengers gathered from the nearby river landing, board the train, and at 9 o'clock sharp to the accompaniment of a cheer and shouts of good wishes from the whole Steveston population the engineer turned on the steam, and the train made up of five first class coaches and an observation car, moved slowly out.

The first stop was made at the contractor's camp to take on a number of the men who have been working on the line, and who, at the expense of their employer, all enjoyed a well deserved holiday. The journey from this point is not all interesting, in a scenic sense. The country is flat in the immediate vicinity, and never can offer any great inducement to the sight-seeing tourist. But that, however, is the last thing thought of in the line laying.

The opening up of one of the most fertile tracts of farming land in the province, being the recognized necessity that compelled the construction of the Lulu Island Railway. That this line was needed, there can be no doubt, thousands of acres of farming land hitherto dependent on stage coach and wagon connection with Vancouver, are now tapped in their very richest parts, and what is more important than all to the dairy farmer, the markets can now be reached in about half an hour as against some three hours in the old way.

The first stop is at Inglewood township [the early Bridgeport area] and immediately beyond it the train comes over the Arm on a high trestle bridge, and a half mile beyond, Eburne Station is reached. Past it a cut is made through a more elevated country and dense bush. Magee Road [now 49th Avenue in Vancouver] is soon passed, and although no stop was made here, at this point a station will be placed in the near future. From this on to Vancouver a few more stopping places are passed, and in Vancouver itself, several stops are made at convenient points before the general terminus is reached.

The whole journey was made in one and a quarter hours, which considering the fact that the track has only been finished for a few days, should be reckoned pretty good time.

Cannery workers used the line extensively as this first rail service replaced the much slower horse drawn stages. The CPR Sockeye Limited ran from Granville up the 16th Avenue hill and through the forests, often dropping off supplies for the logging camps along the way.

While the primary purpose was to carry cannery workers, the Company began advertising for tourists to take a day trip to Steveston and the canneries.

According to *New Westminster's Past* — a 1902 reference:

Residents of Vancouver, as well as the City's visitors, became cannery tourists that summer, when the Canadian Pacific Railway opened its Lulu Island branch line and operated twice daily runs to Steveston and return. As well as providing a popular sightseeing trip, the train proved of inestimable convenience to the Lulu Island community, and was so well patronized generally that it soon became dubbed the "Sockeye Limited". The Canadian Pacific Railway operated this line until July 4, 1905 when the BC Electric Company inaugurated its tram service.

The Way We Were by the staff of the *Province* newspaper notes that in 1902 "the first passenger train arrives in Steveston to serve the canneries. It becomes known as the *Sockeye Express.*"[1]

Note: All references to the CPR's train service to Steveston was referred to by the company as the *Sockeye Limited*. While the BCER service to Steveston was dubbed The *Sockeye Special* because the bulk of their morning and afternoon passengers were cannery workers whose mainstay was the processing of sockeye salmon. Other than the newspaper reporter's story, the *Sockeye Express* was never used or adopted by either the CPR or the BCER.

At the turn of the century, the opening of the fishing season in Steveston was celebrated by thousands. The CPR operated passenger trains to Steveston while paddle wheelers came down the Fraser River from New Westminster.

Sternwheelers *Brunswick* and *George Star* operated between New Westminster and Steveston for a 25 cent fare. Stops were made along the river when a resident raised a flag on the shore line. By 1923, the *George Star* was the only sternwheeler offering this service.

Sternwheeler *Transfer*
Philip Timms photo,
Vancouver Public Library
VPL 7321

---

1 White, Silas, ed. *The Way We Were: BC's Amazing Journey to the Millennium.* (Vancouver: Vancouver Province, 2000), 19.

Crowds of 10,000 to 15,000 would travel from Vancouver, New Westminster and surrounding areas with their picnic lunches and tents to socialize and witness the spectacular opening of the fishing season. At 6 o'clock on a Sunday evening, the rocket gun would go off. There was somebody standing with a little rocket gun every so far along on the river and one could see the smoke in the air as the rocket went off which signaled the start of the fishing season.

Fishing boats
City of Richmond Archives, Photograph #1978.34.40

All the fishermen used rowboats or sailboats and the sound of corks (cedar floats) dropping overboard, there was no noise, just the sound of the corks. Government boats patrolled the river to enforce the fishing regulations.

The Steveston line, however, didn't prove to be a money maker for the CPR because the canneries preferred to ship their goods on the large sailing ships since the major markets were overseas. After three years of operation, the line was taken over by the young BC Electric Railway Co.

10

Chapter II

The BC Electric Railway Co.

The Westminster and Vancouver Tramways Company was incorporated April 26, 1890; and a train line between Vancouver and New Westminster was put into service in June of the same year. Due to the depression in 1891 as well as the defaulting of the Company's bonds, WCTCo. was taken over by the bond holders in 1893. In April 1895 the Consolidated Railway and Light Corporation purchased the assets.

By April 1897, the assets were assumed by the new company, the B.C. Electric Railway Company. This takeover included the line between New Westminster and Vancouver known as the Central Park Interurban.

The early *Richmond* car and crew
City of Richmond Archives, Richmond car

In 1905, the BCER leased the CPR lines and the electrification of the Vancouver & Lulu Island Railway was underway. Having taken less than three months, the trial date for electric locomotion was set for June 26, 1905. The new *Eburne* car (later numbered 1206) was chosen as the vehicle to take the official party on a slow running inspection tour over the whole of the line.

Freight traffic used the line so the interurban would receive a clearance form stating that the interurban car was to be met at a certain station. Freight engines did not receive any clearances and their crews reported to the Station Agent that they were headed for Eburne, Steveston or another point and they would wait for the first car to come along and send a brakeman out as a flagman.

There was a telephone connection at every station and each car carried a portable telephone which could be used along the line as every tenth pole was equipped to handle a telephone connection.

The *Eburne* and her equally new sisters, *Steveston* (later 1207) and *Richmond* (later 1205) were completed by the New

1918 Steveston tram and crew
City of Richmond Archives, Photograph #1978 21 36

Westminster shop crews just barely in time for the beginning of service on the new line. They were identicfal to the five named interurban's running on the Westminster branch, except that the fourteen windows on each side, were grouped into pairs of seven upper windows with colored glass, and the non-smoking and smoking sections seated 32 and 24 respectively, rather than 36 and 20.

The *Eburne*, in her resplendent B.C. Electric coat of jade green, with gold trim and black undercarriage, attracted much attention on her first run, and although the substation was not yet ready, power was supplied from Vancouver.

Return fare from Vancouver to Eburne was 40¢ and to Steveston and back 85¢. On Sundays and holidays, the fares were 30¢ and 75¢. Commercial travelers paid 60¢ for the Vancouver to Steveston trip, while clergymen paid half fare. During the rush hour, there was half-hourly service between Vancouver and Eburne.

The line's stately cars had smoking and non-smoking sections and the *Richmond*, *Steveston* and *Eburne* did much to open up the land between Sea Island and Steveston becoming

Tram interior with cane seats and smoking section at rear
Ron Schuss Collection

an important part of both the economic and social life of Lulu Island

Leaving the car barns in Vancouver, the tram proceeded south through Kerrisdale and Eburne (later named Marpole) before crossing the Fraser River on the CPR railway bridge. On Lulu Island, the tram proceeded on the leased CPR tracks along Garden City Road (in early years it was called Railway Avenue North) curving onto Granville Avenue then onto Railway Avenue South. These two junctions had long curves since the original CPR tracks were designed for multi-boxcar trains.

The "staff" (a 12" piece of dowling) was used for a year or two on a single track line. The motorman would "see the staff" giving permission for the first tram to go. If there was more than one train on the line, for example passenger and freight, the flagman for each train held the "staff" passing it to the next train for authority to proceed.

At the end of the line, the trams did not turn around but just reversed direction. The conductor flipped the cane seat backs so passengers would face the front and the motorman pulled the power trolley down from the back car going in and put the power trolley up on the back car going out.

Eburne Bridge 1908
Philip Timms photo, Vancouver Public Library VPL 2128

The original Vancouver depot at the foot of Granville Street at the west end of the Kitsilano Trestle, was later moved to the old Granville Street Bridge. Under pressure from the City of Vancouver it was later moved to Seymour and Davie Streets.

Operating out of the Davie Street Station, trams of the Steveston line used the streetcar line out of the city, until entering a private right-of-way, then proceeding on a double track from Vancouver to Marpole, from there it continued to Steveston at sixty minute intervals.

The stations of the Lulu Island branch in 1913 and the miles from the Vancouver depot were:

6.5	Eburne Junction
7.3	Tucks
7.7	Sexsmith
8.0	Bridgeport
8.3	Cambie
8.5	Alexandra
8.8	Rifle Range
9.5	Garden City
10.2	Brighouse
11.2	Lulu
12.2	Blundell
13.0	Woodwards
13.6	Branscombe
14.0	Steveston Wye
14.5	Steveston

British Columbia's "keep to the left" was one of the last holdouts on the North American continent. On July 1, 1920, "right rule of the road" became effective in British Columbia except for the Coast Region where all the large cities were located.

The BCER, Vancouver, Victoria and New Westminster and other lines totaling 366 miles of track with the mechanical changes and heavy costs involved, justified the delay to changeover to January 1, 1922. The single item of special steel for cross overs and other track changes on the mainland was $700,000. The government offered to pay half the cost provided their share was not more than $350,000.

The BC Electric Railway Company had their Mechanical Department undertake alterations but as most cars had their steering wheel on the left, the change went smoothly.

Other modifications

- they had to build new steps on the right side and remove those on the left
- the Maintenance-of-way Department had to undertake alterations to track and stations
- the Electrical Department had to change overhead wiring
- the Traffic Department had to train its personnel.

1922 BCER Maintenance Crew
Buzzer Vol. 40 No. 16
City of Richmond Archives

It was impossible to change cars completely for the right hand rule. Partial changes were made quickly so that a minimal number of cars were removed from service and returned as soon as possible. Time could not be spared for paint to dry so parts were made separately and painted before installation.

Switches had been worn in one direction and rough corners often projected, tending to throw the cars off the track. The cars used slower speeds on curves to keep them on the tracks.

While the Marpole/Eburne bridge was usually closed to accommodate the crossing for the very busy schedule of trains, boats would blow their airhorn for the bridge to open so they could proceed up and down the river.

The bridges were opened by hand through a series of gears by the Bridge Tender, Mr. Tuck, who lived in a house under the Island end of the long bridge. Mr. Tuck was a colorful character and once accused a tugboat captain of waiting around the bend of the river until the bridge was closed, then hooting his horn as soon as Mr. Tuck was back home.

During the ensuing argument, Mr. Tuck threw a wrench at the tug captain, and then realized he didn't have a wrench to fix the plates back on the rails; there was an investigation.

The low level draw bridge was a challenge for trams to maintain their tight time schedule as countless trams were held up waiting for boats to pass.

Bridge tender's gear house for opening and closing the bridge
Detail of City of Richmond Archives, Cars on bridge

18

Chapter III

Other Transportation Endeavors

The success of the *Sockeye Special*'s Vancouver to Steveston service prompted the Canadian Northern Pacific Railway (CnoPR) to offer a competitive service from New Westminster to Steveston. The CnoPR ran from the Alberta/British Columbia border to Vancouver and was a wholly owned subsidiary of the Canadian Northern Railway (CNoR). The CnoPR was incorporated in 1910 and the last spike was installed at Basque, B.C. (near Ashcroft, B.C. on the historic Basque Ranch) in January 1915. The event completed Canada's third transcontinental railway which ran from Quebec to Vancouver. The CNoR system was nationalized by the Crown in 1918.

In 1912, the Company embarked on a branch line to Lulu Island after purchasing 3,600 feet of water frontage in Burnaby at the 'big bend' on the North Arm of the Fraser River. After crossing the North Arm of the Fraser, the line proceeded for ⅝ mile south along Number 10 Road on Lulu Island to the South Arm of the Fraser River, where at the wye, the main line followed the curve on the south shore to its destination at Steveston. At Steveston, a connection was made with the BCER wye (laid by the CPR in 1902) on Railway Avenue at Moncton Street.

The track sheet in the City of Richmond Archives indicates station buildings in Queensborough, Woodwards Landing and Steveston. These stations were constructed at Port Mann, loaded on flat cars for shipment to Lulu Island, but due to their height, could not pass through the BCER depot and were routed to Vancouver using the Great Northern Railway tracks.

A water tower was built at Woodwards Landing at the south foot of No. 5 Road and a 777 foot siding was located just west of No. 5 Road. One source claims a station existed at Ewen's Landing at the south foot of No. 9 Road, but this cannot be verified. The Ewen Cannery on Lion Island employed many people and this purported landing was a flag stop.

The Canadian Northern Railway arriving at Fort Langley
Langley Centennial Museum, Photo #2665

Seventeen months after the scheduled lightly-used Canadian Northern Pacific Railway Lulu Island Branch service to Steveston began, with peat bogs and burnt trestles, the service ended forever.

Chapter IV

The Development of Lulu Island and its Community

The *Sockeye Special* had a major impact on life and the development on Lulu Island. The interurbans were a very important link in the transportation infrastructure. The faithful trams helped to shape the lives of many families as the historic wooden cars rocked and swayed their way by the green farmlands to Steveston and the canneries.

The Steveston tram and passengers
Philip Timms photo, Vancouver Public Library VPL 2179

The tram's friendly whistle was known to all. People would be awakened by the first tram out in the morning and would be ready to catch the next one to their destination. Those were the days when everyone knew everyone and a trip on the tram was a big family gathering.

Many of the new settlers worked in Vancouver, using the interurban for transportation to get to work. The tram not only carried passengers but also their belongings, such as garden implements, a roll of tarpaper, crated chickens and geese or even a trussed up calf on the rear vestibule of the Steveston bound tram, such occurrences were commonplace.

The daughter of the Gulf of Georgia Cannery's Fire Chief recalls running for the tram in the morning to catch the tram to school while the conductor, standing on the platform, waved her on to run faster as she was usually a bit late.

Richmond's early seal shows a cornucopia of agricultural products indicating that the area was a major breadbasket for the growing metropolitan area.

Small dairy farmers traveled by the interurban to the farmers' market in New Westminster. On one of the trips, a farmer bought a piglet for fifty cents, put it in a gunnysack and headed home, but the pig ate a hole in the sack and ran up and down the aisle of the tram with the farmer in hot pursuit. He caught the piglet, detrained and headed home to his small dairy farm on No. 2 Road south of Blundell. Just another day on the *Sockeye Special*.

In the 1920's, farmers around the north end of No.6 and 7 Roads had no transportation on Lulu Island so they would row across the North Arm of the Fraser River to catch the Marpole — New Westminster tram.

Fresh load of hay
City of Richmond Archives, Mary Thompson photograph #1985.39.154

The BCER also ran freight trains across the Island. The tram crews alternated ticket gathering and commuter camaraderie with stints on the freights — they were railroaders not streetcar men.

Originally the Steveston train stopped at two train stations in Steveston — the CP Rail station at No. 1 near the Imperial Cannery and Moncton Street and the CN station at the foot of Railway Avenue near Britannia Cannery.

Early rural Steveston area
City of Richmond Archives, Photograph #1978.5.7

Both railways hauled lumber from Eburne and New Westminster to Steveston for shipment to Europe. The CPR loaded frozen halibut from the cold storage building at the Imperial Cannery for shipment to the eastern United States.

Sailing ships loading canned salmon from Steveston canneries
City of Richmond Archives, Photograph #1984.17.11

The canneries loaded their cases of canned salmon onto the tall masted sailing vessels lining the cannery docks, where the prized sockeye salmon was destined for Great Britain and Europe. As many of fourteen tall ships were moored at the Steveston wharf to load some of the 837,489 cases of sockeye salmon from the year's bumper catch.

These vessels originated in Great Britain and Europe and as they unloaded their cargo at the many ports on the South Seas and Caribbean Islands, they took on ballast at the islands by loading up with sand from the beaches for their trip up the Pacific Coast to Steveston. On arrival at the canneries, the sand was dumped in the Fraser River.

Over the years, the river was dredged with the sand pumped onto an expanding Shady Island and later onto the Garry Point area. In the late 1950's and 1960's, large hills of white sand covered the Garry Point area. In those days, Garry Point was referred to as "The Sand Dunes" that were eight to ten feet high. The kids who played on "The Dunes" never realized that the lovely white sand had originated in Bermuda, Barbados, Jamaica, and elsewhere.

Early dredge in Richmond
City of Richmond Archives, Phorograph #1978.14.5

Today Garry Point is an attractive respite west of the Steveston Village where people can enjoy a scenic waterfront path, the Japanese garden, kite flying, picnicking, enjoying fish and chips and watching the birds and boats. Park visitors are oblivious from where the sand is buried beneath the grass and under their feet, originated.

Within one year of operation, the BCER had become an integral part of the Lulu Island community and #9 Road station (Steveston Highway) had its own milk stand. The Company offered special rates on agricultural commodities and many farmers used the railway extensively to ship milk, hay and oats.

The same year, a letter was sent to the General Manager of the BCER requesting "settlers' rates" for bona-fide settlers at #9 Road. These rates were commonly given by the Company to early "settlers", and in this case, were $2.50 for ten rides between Vancouver and No. 9 Road.

In the 1906 directory, Solomon Branscombe was listed as one of the settlers on #9 Road. Three years later Branscombe Station was built at Railway and # 9 Road and was typical of the three — sided structures used up and down the line. Trams were running hourly between 6:30 a.m. and 10:30 p.m. while Branscombe Station apparently had more passengers and freight than most of the other stations.

Branscombe Station
City of Richmond Archives, BCER.Branscombe.Station.May.12.1952

There were now a total of eighteen stations along the Lulu Island section of the line and a 1905 regular fare from Vancouver to Steveston was 85¢ return. Ridership for a seven day period in August 1905 was 7,000 [in spring of 1908 ridership was 7-8000 and in September of 1909 it was 28,000]. Most stations were named after families or individuals who donated the land to get the BCER to put in a stop or station.

1909 *Point Grey Gazette* — Eburne News — January 30

Point Grey Gazette news magazine masthead
Marpole Historical Society collection

An announcement which will greatly interest all the residents of Point Grey Municipality has just been made by the BC Electric Railway, being a substantial reduction in the train rates between Vancouver and Eburne and all intermediate points. The new rates will go into effect at once, just as soon as the tickets leave the printer's hands. Fifty rate month tickets will also be issued as in vogue over the New Westminster line, an innovation which will be undoubtedly warmly welcomed.

According to the new rates, single fare between Eburne and Vancouver will be 20¢ instead of 25¢ with a return ticket of 35¢ instead of 40¢. The ten ride settler's tickets will be reduced from $1.25 to $1.00 while the fifty ride month ticket will be $4.00.

Under the present schedule of rates, the cheapest ride between Vancouver and Eburne is 12¢ according to the new fifty ride month tickets, the rate will be cut to 8¢ which is a substantial reduction. The 50 ride month tickets carry transfer privileges to any point in the city and return to the Granville Street station. Under this arrangement, a resident of Eburne can travel from Eburne to Cedar Cottage and return, a distance of 23 miles, for just 16¢.

The announcement comes as a result of a request from the residents of Point Grey Municipality. That the Company so readily consented to the request and that they decided to place such a sweeping reduction before the patrons, is a matter for congratulations and will no doubt go a long way towards establishing better relations between the two parties.

September 12, 1908 *Eburne News*

Eburne News masthead
Marpole Historical Society collection, Sept.12.1908 Vol. 1 No. 25

STEVESTON NOTES

A party of Stevestonites missed the last tram the other night, but having in mind the experience of a countryman of theirs when walking home, they decided not to try it and hired an automobile instead.

Chapter V

Off to the Races

The trains and interurban were a very important link in the transportation infrastructure for the two Lulu Island racetracks. Prior to 1905, the CPR ran special trains to the races. Later the BCER ran "Racing Specials" from Davie Street to Marpole, then directly to the Minoru and Lansdowne racetracks.

Early trams had wooden benches and were open to the elements. Later the wooden cars were divided including a smaller section with wooden seats reserved for smoking patrons. The larger section had wicker seats for more refined patrons.

Normally travelling at 25 miles per hour, the "Racing Specials" usually ran in tandem, with flags flying and bells clanging to distinguish them from the regular runs. Between Granville Depot and Minoru Park the run was a non-stop

Racing Special **waiting behind the grandstand to take passengers home**
City of Richmond Archives, Photograph #1978.12.9

service, except at Eburne Station, where it took approximately 35 minutes to carry upwards of 300 people.

On racing days, "Specials" made several runs two hours ahead of the first post time. On these days, the interurban parked on a siding immediately behind the grandstands and clubhouses, in readiness for the return run.

The Province newspaper ad read:

"25 minute run" BC Electric Railway special race trains leave Carrol Street Depot daily at 1:00, 1:30 and 2 pm direct to the Grandstand. 15 minute service from the Granville Street Station (Marpole).

Brighouse Racetrack opened in 1909 and was originally named Minoru Racetrack after King Edward's horse, a 1909 Epsom Derby winner. Minoru [the horse] was named after the newborn son of Edward's gardener. The track, often described as having the finest racing surface in North America, and was on the land owned by Sam Brighouse, (one of the Three Greenhorns). It was infinitely easier to build than Vancouver's forested east end, it was built in 90 days for approximately $75,000. An estimated 7,000 fans turned out for opening day, August 21, 1909, to begin the first major racing event in the Lower Mainland.

Epson Derby winner Minoru
City of Richmond Archives

The track's surface created a natural bounce — believed to be the result of underlying peat and a perfect mix of clay and alluvial soil. This may be the reason for the numerous Canadian horse racing records.

Most of the fans rode the BCER trams from Vancouver and Marpole, but others arrived in horse drawn carriages, by horseback or by walking for miles along the flat, dusty roads. Originally the bookmaking system was in effect, but bookies were soon abolished and in 1910, pari-mutual machines "iron men" were installed.

Minoru Racetrack 1920
City of Richmond Archives, Photograph #2001.9.20

Pari-mutual betting had been outlawed in many parts of the United States and for a long time, there was no racing between Mexico and British Columbia. Some of the best known horsemen on the continent came to Vancouver and Richmond. In 1914, an unprecedented 90 day meet was held at Minoru.

Charles Hamilton lands his plane at Minoru Racetrack March 25, 1910 for the first airplane visit west of Winnipeg
Ron Hyde collection

This contravened the law and the Attorney-General fined the track $500.

Minoru Racetrack's first eleven years of operation, recorded several historic events witnessed by thousands who traveled by the *Sockeye Special*. On March 25, 1910, the first airplane visit and first flight west of Winnipeg by Charles K. Hamilton who flew his Curtiss pusher biplane to Minoru Park.

The next day he flew to New Westminster and back. He later challenged a horse to a one mile race and much to Hamilton's embarrassment, the horse won by ten seconds probably due to the ⅜ of a mile lead given to the horse.

April 28, 1911 — William Templeton flew a homemade biplane at Minoru. This was the first plane both built and flown over Metropolitan Vancouver. Templeton later became the first Manager of the Vancouver International Airport .

April 24, 1912 — Billy M. Stark made a solo exhibition flight over Minoru. A second flight was scheduled and the BCER, anticipating large numbers of spectators, added nine extra cars to the Lulu Island Route.

Although the bi-plane was not designed to carry passengers, James Hewitt of the *Province* newspaper, was the first airplane passenger in British Columbia.

William Stark in his plane with James Hewitt strapped to the wing in 1912
City of Vancouver Archives, Trans N38

Pilot Stark took the plane up to 600 feet and flew almost 6 miles while Hewitt sat on a board strapped next to the engine as he hung on to the rigging of the plane.

May 24, 1912 — The first parachute jump in Canada was made into Minoru Park by Charles Saunders.

July 31, 1913 — American Aviatrix Alys McKey Bryant became the first woman in Canada to make a solo flight.

She was a member of the Early Birds and began taking flying lessons in the summer of 1912.

American Aviatrix Alys McKey Bryant
Smithsonian Institution Negative #A9965E

August 1919— Vancouver's Ernest C. Hoy took off from Minoru Park for the first flight to cross the Rocky Mountains. The trip took 16 hours and 42 minutes and contained the first airmail delivery across the Rockies.

With the outbreak of the First World War, Minoru closed after the 1914 season. It did not reopen until 1920 when it became Brighouse Racetrack that attracted fans from all parts of North America and every once in a while, movie stars of the day were in attendance.

Brighouse operated for 22 seasons until it finally closed in 1942 when wartime gas rationing forced all racing to be transferred to Hastings Park. Up until 1931, the flat lands in the immediate vicinity of the Brighouse Track around Garden City Road and Cambie Road, were used as ad-hoc landing strips and a makeshift Vancouver airport.

The Lansdowne Racetrack came about because Sam Brighouse's racing charter moved about one mile north along No. 3 Road to Lansdowne Road. The track was built in 1924 by a group of horse people led by Sam Randall and Walter Georghegan under the banner of the West Coast Jockey Club Ltd. The main reason for the new track was that it provided an opportunity to bring more racing dates to the Lower Mainland, since fourteen days were alloted, the same as Brighouse and Hastings Parks.

Charlie Oldfield, the General Manager of Lansdowne Racetrack, recalled the beginnings of the track. "Al McLennan, George Norgan and others came in to help finance the building. Around here, they wanted $1.30 for the inside rails and outside fence. Well, I got our poles up around Haney. I had a friend

Landsdowne Racetrack
City of Richmond Archives, Photograph #1987.92.1

who was a fisherman and I got the poles made into rafts and had him float them down the Fraser River.

"We got a local firm to build the grandstand and I put in the paddock. We only got the license in February and we opened the track on July 9th. I had bought a lot of trees and planted them, and it didn't look too bad."

The grandstand could hold up to 4,500 spectators and the clubhouse seated 1,000 patrons.

Randall named the track after Lansdowne Park, the football field in Ottawa. [Henry Charles Petty-Fitzmaurice — fifth Marquis of Lansdowne — Governor General of Canada]. It helped provide a golden age for racing in B.C. when Austin Taylor's horse "Indian Broom" finished third in the 1936 Kentucky Derby, and came home later that summer for the Golden Jubilee Handicap and won the race worth $5,000. In Canada, this was the second in value only to the King's Plate.

In 1929, Clay Pewitt, a friend of Lansdowne management, unveiled a machine that would bring racing into a new age of accuracy: the electronic starting gate.

After many ups and downs over the years, in 1973, Jack Diamond sold Lansdowne to Woodwards Stores Ltd. for $3 million for the development of a shopping centre. For more of this interesting story, check out www.bchorseracinghalloffame.org/hoofprints_century.htm.

1945 Lansdowne Park Racing form
Marpole Historical Society collection

West Coast Jockey Club Limited Official Programme. Price 15¢
Landsdowne Park Saturday, June 30 – Saturday, June 7
Seventh Day – Saturday, July 7, 1945
Marpole Historical Society collection

Chapter VI

Social and Entertainment

The *Sockeye Special* was a social and entertainment opportunity for residents of Lulu Island and Vancouver. The special racetrack trams to the Minoru and Lansdowne racetracks created an exciting time with their speed, flags flying and whistles blowing creating a social experience for the people attending the races.

On the other hand, a popular Friday or Saturday night event for Lulu Island residents was to take the tram into Vancouver to attend the opera, see a movie or live show at the Pantages or Orpheum, then catch a late *Sockeye Special* home.

The evening trams would be entertaining as there were fewer passengers and fewer stops. The younger motormen would "open 'er up" full throttle with the tram careening down the track at hair raising speeds, lurching and creaking and often it would be referred to as *The Toonerville Trolley*.

Pantages Theatre Acts for the week
Heritage Vancouver Society
Orpheum Theatre, 1929
Stuart Thomson photo, Vancouver Public Library, VPL 11036

The Chinese in Steveston enjoyed going to Vancouver's Chinatown to gamble and play Mah Jong.

The midnight tram returning to Steveston on Saturday night was referred to as *The Peanut Special* as the riders ate lots of peanuts and dropped the shells all over the tram's floors.

However, Steveston was also the place for fun and entertainment. The Steveston Opera House was the site of an annual New Year's Eve dance, where couples danced the night away. The BCER was always part of the community and would put on a special 3 a.m. tram to take the partyers home.

Steveston Opera House, 1890
City of Richmond Archives, RCF109

The Steveston Opera House, located at 2nd Street and Chatham was built by the Steves family, and used for many purposes during the day. It was the first school in Steveston when parents complained about walking their children to the school at No. 2 Road and the dyke, one and one half miles away. St. Anne's Anglican Church held their services here until the Steveston church was built in 1905.

The poet and entertainer E. Pauline Johnson — Tekahionwake was a popular performer at the Opera House.

When performing at the Opera House, It is likely that E. Pauline Johnson recited her poem from *The Ballad of Yaada – A Legend of the Pacific Coast* that reflected her vision of Lulu Island:

There are fires on Lulu Island and the sky is opalescent
With the pearl and purple tinting from the smouldering of peat
And the dream hills lift their summits in a sweeping hazy crescent
With Capilano cañon at their feet.

There are fires on Lulu Island, and the smoke, uplifting lingers
In a faded scarf of fragrance as it creeps across the bay
And the inlet and the narrows blur beneath its silent fingers,
And the cañon is enfolded in its grey.

Pauline E. Johnson (1862-1913)
Cochran, Library and Archives Canada, Acc. no. 1952-010, C-085125

In 1901, a record 16 million pounds of salmon were shipped world-wide from the Steveston canneries. At that time, Steveston was a thriving community, it had an opera house, gambling houses, opium dens, brothels, hotels and saloons serving a population that swelled to 10,000 during the fishing season; this did not include the fishermen or crews from the sailing vessels who were in port loading cases of canned sockeye.

The trams were the main source of transportation as many could not afford a car. The last tram on Saturday night left the Davie Street station at midnight and it was the only link back to Richmond. Invariably, someone would stay too late at a dance hall, bowling alley, movie theatre or skating rink and would make a mad dash down Davie Street just as the last tram was starting to pull out. The conductor would stand outside the tram shouting and waving the last passengers down the street, even those on board cheered as the ongoing passengers ran down the street and breathlessly scrambled aboard.

London Hotel, 1908
City of Richmond Archives, RCF105

Steveston native daughter Dolly Harper reminisced in *Back on Track*:

 BACK ON TRACK

Magazine masthead
Steveston Interurban Restoration Society

In the late 20's, riding on the interurban was one of the highlights of my childhood life. About once a year we traveled all the way from Steveston to North Vancouver, a long trip involving the interurban to Davie Street, the city street car to the North Vancouver ferry and finally a rough ride on the Lynn Valley line to our destination.

Allowing for missed connections, we barely had time for a cup of tea and an envious look at my cousin's collection of Bobbsey Twin books, before it came time to start for home. The scary part was over the trestle bridge beyond Tucks station as there were no guard rails. I expected the train to fall into the river at any moment!

Later memories in the 30's are of High School days when we traveled to Richmond High then on to Cambie Road in double ender cars. The back one was usually full of Japanese, the front a mixture - an unplanned segregation that just happened. We knew all the conductors and motormen by name, Bill Ken, Charlie Martin, Billie Deagle and the father and son Bastion crew to name a few.

Young couples had a challenge for the young man to walk his date home then try to catch the last tram. A lovely recollection:

I remember so many times my date from the city walking me home from the Brighouse tram station. The only trouble was that the same tram that brought us home continued on to Steveston, turned around and headed straight back to Vancouver. This took all of a half an hour and there just wasn't time for an ardent suitor to walk the full mile to my home. A little over half way home, he said a hasty good-night and ran all the way back to the station.

Those wonderful conductors, with a soft spot in their hearts for teenagers of our time, knew just which stations the boys should be returning to. They would wait patiently for a few minutes for the winded passenger to wheeze the last few steps to the station and stagger on board."

Conductor Bill Trew
Private Collection

The *Sockeye Special* and their motormen and conductors were part of the community. Just about everyone knew them and likewise they knew just about everyone. A long time resident recalls, when at five years old, his mother walked him to the tram where he got on by himself for a trip to Marpole to attend kindergarten at St. Anthony's Catholic School.

There were never any concerns as the conductor knew the children and would be certain they got off at the correct station. In 1925 Father Patrick Fogarty established St. Anthony of Padula Parish which included the area south of 49th Avenue (previously Magee Road) between Cambie Street and

MacDonald Avenue including all of Sea Island and Lulu Island west of No. 6 Road. St. Anthony's Catholic School was located at 1345 West 73rd Avenue in Vancouver.

Shared memories include lining pop bottle caps on the track (Orange Crush caps were a favourite with their bright orange color) waiting for the tram to come by and flatten them. Occasionally a penny was put on the track to be flattened, but this did not happen too often because a cent could buy up to ten candies at the local confectionery.

Teenagers would sometimes steal potatoes from a farmer's field, light a fire behind the Alexandra Station, roast the potatoes and give them to the conductor and motorman. Several long time residents reminisced about waiting for the interurban where the conductor and motorman were their friends. They would pay their fare from Branscombe to Vancouver and the conductor would give the full amount back in change.

Chapter VII

The Sockeye Special Family

Many of the motormen and conductors that worked the *Sockeye Special* were members of the Lulu Island community and were widely known by the many passengers that frequented the trams. They knew the families, children and grandchildren. They took their job seriously and loved the camaraderie with their passengers.

Roy and Bert Hall
Ron Schuss collection

Fares were not collected by the motorman, they were paid to a conductor who had to pass through two or more cars. It was a cumbersome collection system. Vic Sharman recalls "a train leaving Marpole Station for Steveston would be at Tucks, the first station, in about three minutes with the conductor still working his way through the first car. Consequently the brakeman in the second car was required to collect fares without the ability to issue receipts. This would go on for several stations until the conductor finally reached the second car. The brakeman, with his pockets full of nickels and dimes, would eventually turn the money over to the conductor."

Vic Sharman
Private collection

A motorman ranked above a conductor or brakeman and, when Vic began working as a conductor, the driver was paid ninety-six and a half cents an hour. In 1946 Vic Sharman moved from Motorman to become BCER Manager of Planning and Scheduling.

John Jackson, retired BCER conductor, wrote in *Back on Track*:

Brownie

Certainly, 'Brownie' was a character. He had been a box-car cowboy in the dirty 30's. Perhaps the term Box-car cowboy needs to be explained. Tens of thousands of young men searching for work, rode the box cars across the country in a futile search for work. Hence the term Box-car cowboy'.

John Jackson
Private collection

In 1942, Brownie found work as a conductor for the British Columbia Electric Railway. He was also a gambler who liked to play the horses and to my knowledge, never picked a winner.

To finance his "love" for playing the horses, he used his "changer" fund. This is money loaned to conductors, one-man car and bus operators, by the BCER company. This "float" was used to give change to passengers, if necessary, after buying a ticket.

Every so often, the company would check "changers" and we, as fellow workers, would loan him a roll of dimes, nickels or quarters. "How did you make out?" we asked. "Oh, I was only $30.00 short" he would say.

The company probably knew what we were doing to bail him out. There were others who did the same thing to finance their after hours beers.

BCER Conductor
Detail of image, private collection

The Lulu Island line was shared by the BCERailway along with the CPR and at Steveston with the CNR. Scheduling was very important to ensure the safety and trouble-free usage by the three railways and the *Sockeye Special*. Detailed time schedules were produced and posted showing the station stops between Vancouver and Steveston with the exact arrival time at each station.

Time cards
Vic Sharman collection

To ensure the accuracy of the tram's arrival at each station, an inspector checked the watch of each conductor every six months and noted any small discrepancy (seconds slow or seconds fast) on the conductor's time card that he was required to carry at all times. With this system, train crews were rarely affected by the *Sockeye Special*'s strict schedule.

No. 1211 with crew
Private collection

British Columbia Elect
TIME T.

SECOND

TAKING EFFECT FIVE

LINE

W. G. MURRIN
President

BCER Timetable No. 71 — March 1, 1945
Vic Sharman collection

Railway Company Ltd.
No. 71

DISTRICT

DAY, MARCH 1, 1945

...inster
...TIME

...i/c of Transportation

J. B. MOUAT
Superintendent.

(ISLAND) SUBDIVISION

THURSDAY, MARCH 1ST, 1945

SOUTH BOUND
— SUPERIOR DIRECTION —
PASSENGER — FIRST CLASS

	210	212	214	216	218	220		222	224	226	228	230	232		234	236	238	240	242	244		246	248	250	252	254	256	258	260	262
Vancouver	DAILY	DAILY EXCEPT SUNDAY	DAILY EXCEPT SUNDAY	DAILY	DAILY	DAILY		DAILY	DAILY	DAILY	DAILY	DAILY	DAILY		DAILY	DAILY EXCEPT SUNDAY	DAILY EXCEPT SUNDAY	DAILY	DAILY	DAILY		DAILY	DAILY EXCEPT SUNDAY	DAILY EXCEPT SUNDAY	DAILY	DAILY	DAILY	DAILY	DAILY	DAILY
.8	5³⁷	6²⁷	6³⁷	7²⁷	7⁵²	8³⁷		9³⁷	10³⁷	11³⁷	12³⁷	13³⁷	14³⁷		15³⁷	15⁵⁷	16³⁷	16³⁷	17²⁷	17⁵⁷		18²⁷	18³⁷	19²⁷	19⁵⁷	20²⁷	21³⁷	22²⁷	23²⁷	24²⁷
.3	5⁵³	6²³	6⁵³	7²³	7⁴⁹	8⁵³		9⁵³	10⁵³	11⁵³	12⁵³	13⁵³	14⁵³		15⁵³	15⁵³	16²³	16⁵³	17²³	17⁵³		18⁵³	18³³	19⁵³	19⁵³	20²³	21⁵³	22²³	23⁵³	24⁵³
.1	5⁵¹	6²¹	6⁵¹	7²¹	7⁴⁷	8⁵¹		9⁵¹	10⁵¹	11⁵¹	12⁵¹	13⁵¹	14⁵¹		15²¹	15⁵¹	16²¹	16⁵¹	17²¹	17⁵¹		18²¹	18⁵¹	19²¹	19⁵¹	20²¹	21²¹	22²¹	23²¹	24²¹
.3	5⁴⁸	6¹⁸	6⁴⁸	7¹⁸	7⁴⁴	8⁴⁸		9⁴⁸	10⁴⁸	11⁴⁸	12⁴⁸	13⁴⁸	14⁴⁸		15¹⁸	15⁴⁸	16¹⁸	16⁴⁸	17¹⁸	17⁴⁸		18¹⁸	18⁴⁸	19¹⁸	19⁴⁸	20⁴⁸	21⁴⁸	22⁴⁸	23⁴⁸	24⁴⁸
.1																														
.7																														
4	5⁴⁶	6¹⁶	6⁴⁶	7¹⁶	7⁴²	8⁴⁶		9⁴⁶	10⁴⁶	11⁴⁶	12⁴⁶	13⁴⁶	14⁴⁶		15¹⁶	15⁴⁶	16¹⁶	16⁴⁶	17¹⁶	17⁴⁶		18¹⁶	18⁴⁶	19¹⁶	19⁴⁶	20²¹	21⁴⁶	22⁴⁶	23⁴⁶	24⁴⁶
4	5⁴⁴	6¹⁴ m211	6⁴⁴ m213	7¹⁴ m215	7⁴⁰ m217	8⁴⁴		9⁴⁴	10⁴⁴	11⁴⁴	12⁴⁴	13⁴⁴	14⁴⁴		15¹⁴ m233	15⁴⁴ m235	16¹⁴ m237	16⁴⁴ m239	17¹⁴ m241	17⁴⁴ m243		18¹⁴ m245	18⁴⁴ m247	19¹⁴ m249	19⁴⁴ m251	20⁴¹	21⁴⁴	22⁴⁴	23⁴⁴	24⁴⁴
9																														
5																														
1	5³⁸	6⁰⁸	6³⁸	7⁰⁸	7³⁷	8³⁸		9³⁸	10³⁸	11³⁸	12³⁸	13³⁸	14³⁸		15⁰⁸	15³⁸	16⁰⁸	16³⁸	17⁰⁸	17³⁸		18⁰⁸	18³⁸	19⁰⁸	19³⁸	20³⁸	21³⁸	22³⁸	23³⁸	24³⁸
8																														
4	5³⁷	6⁰⁷	6³⁷	7⁰⁷	7³⁵	8³⁷		9³⁷	10³⁷	11³⁷	12³⁷	13³⁷	14³⁷		15⁰⁷	15³⁷	16⁰⁷	16³⁷	17⁰⁷	17³⁷		18⁰⁷	18³⁷	19⁰⁷	19³⁷	20³⁷	21³⁷	22³⁷	23³⁷	24³⁷
9	5³⁴	6⁰⁴	6³⁴	7⁰⁴	7³⁴	8³⁴		9³⁴	10³⁴	11³⁴	12³⁴	13³⁴	14³⁴		15⁰⁴	15³⁴	16⁰⁴	16³⁴	17⁰⁴	17³⁴		18⁰⁴	18³⁴	19⁰⁴	19³⁴	20³⁴	21³⁴	22³⁴	23³⁴	24³⁴
6																														
9	5³⁰	6⁰⁰	6³⁰ m211	7⁰⁰ m213	7³⁰ m215	8³⁰ m219		9³⁰ m221	10³⁰ m223	11³⁰ m225	12³⁰ m227	13³⁰ m229	14³⁰ m231		15³⁰	15³⁰	16³⁰	16³⁰	17⁰⁰	17³⁰		18⁰⁰	18³⁰	19⁰⁰	19³⁰ m243	20²⁰ m245	21²⁰ m247	22²⁰ m249	23²⁰ m251	24³⁰ m253
5	5²¹	5⁵¹	6²¹	6⁵¹	7²¹	8²¹		9²¹	10²¹	11²¹	12²¹	13²¹	14²¹		14²¹	15²¹	15⁵¹	16²¹	16⁶¹	17²¹		17²¹	18²¹	18⁵¹	19²¹	20²¹	21²¹	22²¹	23²¹	24²¹
3	5¹⁸	5⁴⁸	6¹⁸	6⁴⁸	7¹⁸	8¹⁸		9¹⁸	10¹⁸	11¹⁸	12¹⁸	13¹⁸	14¹⁸		14⁴⁸	15¹⁸	15⁴⁸	16¹⁸	16⁴⁸	17¹⁸		17⁴⁸	18¹⁸	18⁴⁸	19¹⁸	20¹⁸	21¹⁸	22¹⁸	23¹⁸	24¹⁸
3	5¹³	5⁴³	6¹³	6⁴³	7¹³	8¹³		9¹³	10¹³	11¹³	12¹³	13¹³	14¹³		14⁴³	15¹³	15⁴³	16¹³	16⁴³	17¹³		17⁴³	18¹³	18⁴³	19¹³	20¹³	21¹³	22¹³	23¹³	24¹³
5	5⁰⁵	5³⁵	6⁰⁵	6³⁵	7⁰⁵	8⁰⁵		9⁰⁵	10⁰⁵	11⁰⁵	12⁰⁵	13⁰⁵	14⁰⁵		14³⁵	15⁰⁵	15³⁵	16⁰⁵	16³⁵	17⁰⁵		17³⁵	18⁰⁵	18³⁵	19⁰⁵	20⁰⁵	21⁰⁵	22⁰⁵	23⁰⁵	24⁰⁵
5	5⁰⁰	5³⁰	6⁰⁰	6³⁰	7⁰⁰	8⁰⁰		9⁰⁰	10⁰⁰	11⁰⁰	12⁰⁰	13⁰⁰	14⁰⁰		14³⁰	15⁰⁰	15³⁰	16⁰⁰	16³⁰	17⁰⁰		17³⁰	18⁰⁰	18³⁰	19⁰⁰	20⁰⁰	21⁰⁰	22⁰⁰	23⁰⁰	24⁰⁰
	210	212	214	216	218	220		222	224	226	228	230	232		234	236	238	240	242	244		246	248	250	252	254	256	258	260	262

When passengers had disembarked from the tram and those getting on were seated, the conductor pulled the signal wire that rang in the motorman's area. This signal indicated that it was safe to proceed. This system ensured constant communication between the conductor and the motorman.

The *Sockeye Special* was also dubbed the Father and Son Line as seven different crews consisted of the father being the motorman and his son being the conductor.

Motorman	Conductor
George Boston	George Bostion Jr.
Barr	Len Barr
Demaresq	Demaresq
Bill Moffatt	Moffatt

Boeing Airraft of Canada Ltd. employee button
Tony Miletich collection

During World War II, the tram carried thousands of workers to Marpole station where they transferred to busses to the Boeing construction factory on Sea Island. These workers became part of the regulars and could be easily identified with their worker's badge.

Many of the workers lived in the Burkeville community on Sea Island, in houses built for them by Boeing. After the war and the closing of the Boeing plant, the houses were designated for returned soldiers.

In 1943, the BCER hired women to work on transit because of the labour shortage during the war. With gas rationing, public transportation was more popular than ever and the number of passengers per day increased from 150,000 in January 1938 to over 270,000 by March 1943.

The women hired during this period were called "conductorettes". They worked only on Vancouver streetcar routes — you would not find them on the interurbans. This was a male domain.

BCER also hired women to work as "Electric Guides" selling pre-sold tickets at busy streetcar stops in Vancouver.

The war made many changes to life in Vancouver as women were recognized as an important part of the workforce.

BC Electric Advertisement
Private collection

50

Chapter VIII

The Sockeye Special and the Dairy Industry

For the many dairy farms on Lulu Island, the BCER and the *Sockeye Special* helped the dairy farmers of Richmond compete with the Vancouver milk producers by transporting milk into the city at lower rates and on a regular basis.

J. Thompson's barn and cattle, 1923
City of Richmond Archives, Mary Thompson photo 1985.39.147

Manoah Steves Dairy wagon ca 1905
City of Richmond Archives, 1988.37.39

Manoah Steves imported the first herd of Holsteins in 1889 and by 1900 most farmers had their own cows supplying milk for their families and for sale to the Vancouver dairies.

Richmond's head start as Vancouver's major milk supplier did not last long. In 1909 the BCER established a line to Chilliwack giving the Fraser Valley direct access to the Vancouver market.

This resulted in chaotic marketing with dairies co-operating to blacklist defiant farms. The price of milk dropped from two dollars a can to one dollar.

Milk producers banded together to form the Fraser Valley Milk Producers' Association. The signers from Richmond of the original 1913 charter were D.E. McKay, George McClelland and J.B. McLean.

By 1917, the Association formally began its business activity and the Richmond membership had increased substantially. The monthly meetings of the Richmond local were held in the Eburne Post Office starting on November 3, 1917.

The 1920s, platforms were built at the Sexsmith and Branscombe stations that would hold sixty ten gallon milk cans, weighing 129 lbs each when full. Farmers shipped their

BCER Advertisement promoting shipping milk on their trains and trams
Private collection

milk to Vancouver in the early morning and each night the trams returned their milk cans with names attached, filled with spring water from Marpole. Fresh drinking water was a precious commodity to the Islanders before the first wooden mains were installed to pipe in water from the mainland. Water also came from the Marpole spring in 18 gallon tubs.

The London Family farmouse — note the water tower at the back left
City of Richmond Archives, Photograph #1984.17.74

Depending on the tides Lulu Island was often lower than the water level. Thus Richmond never had wells since the water would be saline. Household water came from rain barrels or returned milk cans. Water for the animals and crops came from the many drainage ditches and canals that criss-crossed the island.

Grauer barns, 1923
City of Richmond Archives, Photograph #1985.39.150

The 1938 Richmond Directory listed nine dairies on Lulu and Sea islands:

Ascot Fair Dairy	335 Steveston Highway	
Beecham's Dairy	356 Blundell Rd	W.E. Beecham
Brentwood Farm Dairy	208 River Road	Amos Fish
Brooksband Dairy Farm	328 River Road	
Brown's Dairy	305 Brown Road	Roy Brown
Frasea Dairy Farm	225 Grauer Road	Jake Grauer
H.P. Dairy Farm	284 No. 4 Road	
University Dairy	No. 5 Road	
Wilford Dairy	82 Westminster Hwy	G. Bennett

The BCER saw the opportunity to increase their shipping traffic by supplying electricity to the many farms on the eastern half of Lulu Island. The Lulu Island dairy industry continued to grow.

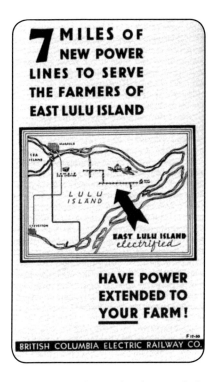

BCER ad promoting electric hookup to their system
Private collection

56

Chapter IX

Rails to Rubber: The Ongoing Demise of the Streetcars and Trams in Greater Vancouver

The success of the system operated by the BC Electric Railway was quietly under attack. In 1922 Alfred P. Sloan Jr., the genius behind General Motors, devised a business strategy to expand automobile sales and to maximize profits by eliminating streetcars. According to General Motors' files, Sloan established a special unit within the Company that was charged, among other things, with the task of replacing America's electric railways with cars, trucks and buses.

In December, 1925, BC Electric saw the need to extend the unified service on the south side of the Fraser. Thus another subsidiary called BC Rapid Transit Company Ltd. was formed.

Early Pacific Stage Lines bus to White Rock
Miss Simpson from Pitt Meadows was a regular on the run
Surrey Historical Society

It absorbed Goodman Hamre's Vancouver to Abbotsford operation, purchased modern buses and extended the route to Chilliwack. The White Star Motor Line, having introduced a service in 1918 between Vancouver and Ladner, was taken over in 1926. Beginning in 1927, a route was established between Vancouver and the resort community of Harrison Hot Springs. This began as a summer only service but was developed into a daily Vancouver-Haney-Mission-Harrison route. A route from Vancouver to Horseshoe Bay, via the Second Narrows Bridge, evolved as soon as the Marine Drive highway was constructed. The operating name of all these services became know as Pacific Stage Lines.

Pacific Stage Lines logo
Private collection

In preparation for this continent-wide change in the transportation business, Chevron opened a refinery in North Burnaby. In 1946, General Motors' 1922 "Rails to Rubber" plan successfully convinced the Canadian and U.S. governments to use taxpayer dollars for car and bus road construction. In contrast, the privately owned BC Electric Railway was alone responsible for the costs of the streetcar and tram tracks, roadbeds, wires, poles, etc., not the taxpayer.

For interesting chronology to transit in the Lower Mainland visit the website:

www.urbanstudio.sala.ubc.ca/2010/readings/transitsolution.pdf

Seeing the various levels of governments and city councils joining the General Motors sponsored band wagon, the BCER placed a street car ad in the *Province* newspaper 29 May 1941:

DOWNTOWN SHOPPERS COME BY STREET CAR

MR. MERCHANT, want to know how your customers travel to your store?

We made an analysis of street car and bus passengers in Vancouver for last November, January and February. We took the ordinary weekdays, eliminating holidays and special sale days.

This was the result:

  Mondays 170,757
  Tuesdays 167,673
  Wednesdays 160,777
  Thursdays 173,716
  Fridays   172,704
  Saturdays 205,749

It will be seen that Wednesday the half-holiday and therefore the day when there is least shopping, has the lowest traffic and Saturday, the acknowledged best shopping day has the highest traffic.

Is any further proof necessary that shoppers travel by street car? If so, here it is:

On ordinary Mondays, street cars and buses carry an average 116,751 passengers; on sale Mondays, we carry an average of 193,207 passengers, nearly 23,000 more, all of whom must be shoppers.

The number of workers using street cars and buses to go to work is practically constant. Authorities estimate that one-quarter of any city's population goes to work each day. On this basis, about 70,000 persons in Vancouver got to work daily. As most of these travel by street car twice, this accounts for a daily travel of 140,000, indicating that all in excess are shoppers or other casual travellers.

It is obvious that the fluctuation of daily travel must be mostly shoppers, the number being only slightly affected by special shows, gatherings and attractions.

The significance of these figures needs hardly be pointed out to the downtown retail merchant. It is that it would be in his own interests to help the mass transportation service in every

EATON'S

way possible because it brings customers to his store.

The private automobile undoubtedly brings some customers downtown, but the numbers are insignificant compared with those who travel by street car. One street car, for example, carries as many Persons as thirty automobiles. Two automobiles take up as much space as one street car, although the former carry only 3.4 persons (by national average) compared with 50 to 90 for the street car.

The street car is the anchor which keeps the downtown business and shopping section where it is. Only the street car can carry the tens of thousands of workers and shoppers in and out of the business section. Without the street car, there would be intolerable congestion of traffic and inevitable decentralization of shopping.

Passengers boarding streetcars
City of Richmond Archives, Ted Clark Fonds

Here, then, are some of the ways retail merchants can assist the street railway system to serve them:

Press for recognition of the street car as the vehicle best suited for mass transportation and see that it receives fair treatment accordingly.

Promote faster street car service by getting for the street car the right-of-way, better loading zones, less restricting legislation.

Eliminate curb parking on downtown car-line streets. Streets were made for moving traffic and it is much more important that the 170,000 to 200,000 street car passengers a day be accommodated than the few automobile owners who can park at the curb.

Help the street railway to serve you better by seeing that it receives an adequate return for its service and that it be not put to unnecessary expense in rendering that service.

Make the street car service your business because the street car rider is your customer.

In 1946, BC Electric released ridership figures for the previous year. Their streetcar and bus service carried 156,091,301 passengers for the year and of these 153,046,000 traveled by streetcar or tram and 3,045,000 traveled by bus. The BC Transit History page shows that in 2008 shows the system of 850 buses carried a ridership of 45,000,000 or 111 million less passengers than 62 years ago.

The various streetcar lines and interurban lines were gradually decommissioned with tracks and roadbeds removed. The streetcars were replaced by a diesel polluting fleet of buses, fouling Vancouver's fresh sea air with diesel exhaust fumes.

The final tram service to go was the Lulu Island line and on February 28, 1958 the four remaining operating interurban trams in British Columbia made their last trip from Steveston to Vancouver. The specially decorated four-car tram comprising cars 1208, 1207, 1231 and 1222 saluted customers along the route.

As the tram left Steveston on its final journey, people waved and cheered with tears in their eyes knowing that Lulu Island would never again hear the click-clack of the wheels on the track, the whistle letting you know the tram was leaving the last station or the friendly smiles and waves of the conductors and motormen who became an integral part of the Island and its way of life and history. Steveston's and Lulu Island's era of trams had disappeared.

The last tram leaving Marpole Station
City of Richmond Archives, BCER 1208.1207.1231.1232.Marpole Stn.Feb.28.1958

THE PRESIDENT AND DIRECTORS OF THE
BRITISH COLUMBIA ELECTRIC COMPANY LIMITED
REQUEST THE COMPANY OF

Mrs J. Cheverton

at a last ceremonial run of the Marpole-Steveston
Interurban Passenger Trains, to be
followed by a luncheon in the Brighouse United Church Hall,
816 Granville, Richmond, B. C.
on February 28, 1958

R.S.V.P.
Miss S. Gray
970 Burrard Street
MU 3-8711, Local 3251

Last Run—See Attached
Timetable
Luncheon—12:15

Invitation to Mrs. J. Cheverton to the last ceremonial run
City of Richmond Archives
Special Train.2

The ceremonial last run is for invited guests only. The train will leave Marpole at 11 a.m. sharp, proceeding to Brighouse, to pick up guests, continuing on to Steveston, and then back to Brighouse. Following the luncheon guests will be returned to their points of boarding either by train or bus.

SPECIAL TRAIN SCHEDULE

Marpole	Lv.	11:00 a.m.
Brighouse	Ar.	11:15
	Lv.	11:20
Steveston	Ar.	11:30
	Lv.	11:45
Brighouse	Ar.	11:55

Train may be boarded at Marpole, Brighouse or Steveston, whichever is most suitable.

Ceremonial last run schedule of stops
City of Richmond Archives
Special Train.1

Last tram travelling through Steveston
City of Richmond Archives, Marpole.Steveston.Final.Run

Roy Hall - passing of the tram to the bus
Ron Schuss Collection

The offical last tram — Bert Hall on right
Ron Schuss collection

Bert Hall and the last tram from Steveston
Ron Schuss collection

The Sockeye Special track, abandoned, but not forgotten.
Private collection

Chapter X

The Richmond Heritage Railroad Society

The Richmond Heritage Railroad Society (RHRS) was formed and registered in November 2003 by a group of Richmond citizens who wanted to ensure that Steveston's heritage tram was preserved and operated in the area.

The Society's mission was "to support and raise funds through memberships, donations, grants and sponsorships in order to promote and contribute to the design, construction and operation of a railroad to accommodate a tram, associated buildings and related improvements, linking heritage sites and other visitor attractions within the City of Richmond." Membership was over 100 within a year.

The goal of the Society was to raise the necessary funds to establish a route, to design and construct a rail bed with track and ultimately find another non-profit group to operate the tram. There never was any intention to obtain or operate a tram but rather to partner with a different non-profit group.

The Steveston Interurban Restoration Society was doing an excellent job restoring the tram 1220, which operated as the *Sockeye Special*, but prospects to ultimately operate it were not promising. The City's projections of $7 - $8 million to provide the road bed, tracks, wiring, etc. seemed insurmountable. The commitment by the RHRS to undertake fund raising and construction of the route never seemed to be recognized by all Council members, although there was ongoing support from the Mayor and some of the Councillors at that time.

The RHRS researched and reviewed the operation of the Nelson Tramway Society who operate a restored streetcar for tourists during the spring and summer months. The car barn is the start of the track in a city park. The track wends its way past an upscale motel, through the parking lot of the Chahko Mika Mall that includes Walmart, Shoppers Drug Mart and Save-On-Foods, then terminates at a roundabout adjacent to the Prestige Lakeside Resort and Conference Centre.

Chahko Mika Mall parking lot, Nelson B.C.
Richmond Heritage Railroad Society

Although safety is rigorously enforced, there seems to be little concern about noise, unsightly wires or mothers with baby buggies. Streetcar 23 is a piece of Nelson history that residents cherish and promote as a great tourist attraction with ridership from throughout the province, from the rest of Canada and internationally.

The Portland streetcar system was also reviewed for up-to-date specifications and costs associated with installing track, wiring, electrical service, etc. The Society endeavored to accumulate accurate statistics and information in order to counter the misinformation about the $7 - $8 million project cost. The Society also endeavored to correct the misinformation about the high costs and high taxes that appeared in local press, letters to the Editor and before City Council.

RHRS found it almost impossible to break through the wall of indifference even though the Society endeavored to clarify its mandate to raise the project funding without any costs to the City or higher taxes.

The Sockeye Special car No. 1220 passing another tram
City of Richmond Archives, Photograph #1999 4 1832, Ted Clark Fonds

The proposed elevated skytrain system for Richmond presented new opportunities. In August 2004, the RHRS Board approved advocacy of an engineering "split level" study of the Richmond section of the RAV line.

By September, 2004, the Society received a draft of the Richmond Streetcar Feasibility Study by URS Engineering of Portland Oregon.

The study looked at the concept of an elevated RAV line terminating at Bridgeport Road and converting the already existing B-Line exclusive bus route on No. 3 Road, into an at-grade streetcar system. The Richmond Council strongly supported an on-grade option along No. 3 Road.

The budget for the elevated portion from Bridgeport Road to the City Centre was $200 million, while an at-grade system for the same route was $62 million. An additional option was to extend the at-grade system along Granville Avenue and down the right-of-way on Railway Avenue. This extension from City Centre to Steveston had a projected cost of $110 million. For the $200 million budget for a RAV from Bridgeport to City Centre, an at-grade system could provide service from Bridgeport Road to Steveston for slightly less than the RAV costs.

The RHRS reviewed the at-grade option with the bidders of the Richmond RAV line, and they concurred with the budget figures and using the RAV budget of $200 million, they would include the construction of an at-grade service to Steveston plus finance the RHRS cost to install the track and services to operate a restored tram. Unfortunately the Translink Board were unbending in their RAV mindset and would not consider the City's desire for an at-grade service.

Steveston Heritage Tram Project Linking the Past with the Future
A partnership proposal presented to RAVxpress by the Richmond Heritage Railroad Society

Working with the RHRS and the City, developer Dana Westermark of London Landing Development Corporation, offered to supply a building at his London Landing development, to house a tram when not in use, a warm, dry environment for repairs and maintenance as well as a meeting room upstairs. The building design was for a drive through when the tram was in service from London Farm to Britannia Heritage Shipyards. It was never proposed "as a static display for the tram" as purported by several opposition groups.

The ensuing months saw countless meetings, newspaper articles and letters to the editor with grossly incorrect information. Council meetings were loaded with residents from the water front apartments claiming the tram would reverberate with noise levels to that of a 747, mothers with babies in buggies and pets petrified as the tram roared up behind them threatening life and limb. The threat of massive tax increases to cover the $10 million dollar cost of installing and maintaining the tram route and interrupting the peace and tranquility that they wished to enjoy after moving to Steveston.

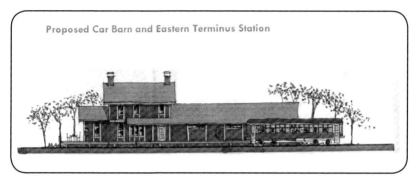

Proposed Car Barn and Station at London Landing
Richmond Heritage Railroad Society brochure

The RHRS had repeatedly responded to these falsehoods confirming the Society's original mission to supply the funding and arranging for the installation of the tram line and services. The tram's speed, like those in Vancouver and Nelson, is to be slightly above the average walking speed.

The original rezoning application by BC Packers for their property, included the route and design of a tram right-of-way along the waterfront, was included in the final rezoning approval by the City.

Space Allowed for a Proposed Heritage Tram

A tram corridor has been incorporated into the development plan. The tram could serve as an exciting historic component of the site and the Steveston waterfront.

At the final Council meeting to review the presentation for the proposed tram operation, an organized NIMBY group was making inroads with some of the Councillors. Councillor Harold Steves made a brilliant last ditch effort with a proposal to operate a tram between Britannia Heritage Shipyards and London Heritage Farm. The route was on City-owned property with the track from Britannia Heritage Shipyards to the boat basin near No. 2 Road that was behind the fence along Bayview Street on the Harbour Board property. One resident from the townhouse development 200 feet away, raised his concerns about the noise and unsightly wires from the tram installation. Immediately one councillor made a motion that no tram shall ever run in Steveston and the tram be a static display.

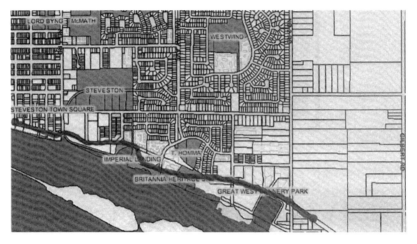

Proposed route of tram linking the Steveston heritage sites
Richmond Heritage Railroad Society

The motion was carried and, with the complaint of a single person, the 100 year history of the *Sockeye Special* and the RHRS mission to preserve its history was closed forever.

The RHRS presented a cheque for $3,000 (the balance of their account) to the author to assist with the writing, publication, promotion and sale of a book on the history of the *Sockeye Special*

This book is the result of this partnership and it is hoped you have enjoyed reading about the *Sockeye Special* and its participation in the growth and community spirit of Lulu Island.

The City of Richmond subsequently purchased the tram for $400,000 from the Steveston Interurban Restoration Society. A early 'tram station style' building is to be constructed at the Corner of No. 1 and Moncton and will become a static display of the *Sockeye Special*.

Car #1220
City of Richmond Archives, Ted Clark Fonds

References

Oral Histories & Interviews

Ball, Gordie — Steveston
Blair, Auleen — oral history — Richmond City Archives
Chandler, Frances and Rex — oral history — Richmond City Archives.
Douglas, Jean — long time Steveston resident and Steveston schoolgirl
Farrell, Dan — Records Analyst — City of Richmond Archives
Gresko, Jacqueline
Hall, Bert — BCER Conductor
Hall, Roy — BCER Motorman
Harper, Dolly — Steveston
Jackson, John — BCER conductor, SIRS
Kacer, John — oral history — City of Richmond Archives
Lang, Richard — oral history — City of Richmond Archives
McNulty, Bill — Steveston writer, historian & Richmond Councillor
McAuley, Eleanor — Quesnel
McManus, D.
Miletich, Tony — Steveston — SIRS
Northey, Jim — long time Richmond resident
Pugsley, Ed — BCER conductor
Purver, Bill, Archivist — City of Richmond Archives
Ransford, Robert — oral history — City of Richmond Archives
Sanford, Jamie
Steves, Harold, writer, historian, Richmond Councillor
Stewart, Janet
Stradiotti, Aldo — oral history — City of Richmond Archives
Van Dusen, Wilfred — oral history — City of Richmond Archives
West, Lois (Midge) — SIRS, Steveston resident
Wilkinson, J. — oral history — City of Richmond Archives
Yarmish, Joe — oral history — City of Richmond Archives

Other Resources

Back on Track, newsletter published by the Steveston Interurban Restoration Society, various issues.
Belshaw, John. "A Day at the Races in Richmond." *Richmond Review*, 1976.
B.C. Horse Racing Hall of Fame
BCER Buzzer — Vol. 40 No. 16 — Vol. 43 No. 8
BCER employees magazine
Brighouse District — Self guided tour — Richmond Museum
Brown, Jack. "The Historical Geography of South Surrey BC." M.A. thesis, Bellingham, WA: Western Washington University, 1971.
Cleeland, Dellis. "Early Transportation." Richmond Nature Park, 1972.
Davis, Chuck — The History of Vancouver
Dawe, Alan. *Richmond and its Bridges — Fifteen Crossings of the Fraser River.* City of Richmond Archives, 1976.

Ewert, Henry. *The Story of the B.C. Electric Railway Co.* Toronto: Whitecap Books, 1986.

Gilker, Gerry, Geraldine Wary; and John M. Lowe. *Whispers from the Shedrows: A History of Thoroughbred Racing in Richmond a Collection of Memoirs and Writings.* Richmond: City of Richmond Archives, 2001.

Heritage Vancouver

Horse Racing Hall of Fame website

Hynek, Barb. "Early Flights in Minoru Park." *Richmond Review,* 1976.

Joannearnottblogspot.com

Johnson, Eric L. *The Canadian Northern*

Leaming, Ruth. "The Proud History of Dairying in Richmond." *Richmond Review,* 1976.

Lee, Jacqueline and Donna Sturmanis, eds. *Richmond, secrets & surprises: A portrait of Richmond in art, photographs, and personal tales.* Richmond, B.C.: Yorklin & Associates, 1994.

London Heritage Farm Society

Lyons, Cicely. *Salmon: our Heritage, the story of a Province and an Industry.* Vancouver: Mitchell Press, 1969.

Marpole Historical Society — Special Collection

MacLachlan, Morag. "The Success of the Fraser Valley Milk Producers' Association." *BC Studies,* no. 24, Winter 1974–75.

"Pacific Railway on Lulu Island" *Point Grey Gazette, Eburne News.*

"Electric Road to Steveston" *The Province,* January 20, 1905.

Phillips, Greg. "A Good Friend Lost — the story of the interurban tram from Steveston to Vancouver." History 21-110-30 working tour submitted to Professor Jacqueline Gresko

The way we were. Vancouver, B.C. Harbour Publishing, 2000.

Reuss, David E. *Fraser Rails That Glow.* Toronto: Whitecap Books, 1986.

Richmond Heritage Railroad Society

Richmond Museum Society

Richmond Review newspaper

Schuss, Ron — SIRS, RHRS, personal collection

Sharman, Vic — SIRS, BCER, personal collection

Smedman, Lisa. *Vancouver: Stories of a City.* The Vancouver Courier, 2008.

St. Anthony of Padua website

Stacey, Duncan and Susan Stacey. *Salmonopolis — The Steveston Story.* Madeira Park, B.C.: Harbour Publishing, 1994.

Steveston Historical Society

Steveston Interurban Restoration Society — *Back on Track*

Surrey Historical Society

Surrey History website, www.surreyhistory.ca.

The Sandhouse Issue 98 Vol. 25 No. 2

The Transit Museum Society newsletter

UBC Main Library — Special Collections

URS Corporation, Portland, Oregon, Engineering study

Browne, Tom. "I remember the trams....," *Vancouver Sun*, November 12, 1971.

Vancouver The Golden Years 1900 — 1910. The Vancouver Museums and Planetarium Association, 1971.

Victoria Colonist, 1905.

78

Index

A

airplane, 32
Ascot Fair Dairy, 54
Ashcroft, B.C., 19

B

B.C. Electric, 13
barns, 51, 54
Basque, B.C., 19
Basque Ranch, 19
Bastion, 41
BC Electric, 61
BC Electric Company, 7
BCER, 8, 9, 11, 12, 15, 16, 19, 20, 23, 25, 26, 30, 32, 38, 43, 44, 48, 51, 52, 55, 57, 58, 59, 75, 76
BCERailway, 44
BC Packers, 71
BC Rapid Transit Company Ltd., 58
Beecham, W.E., 54
Beecham's Dairy, 54
Bennett, G., 54
betting, 31
Boeing, 48
box-car cowboy, 44
brakeman, 43
Branscombe, Solomon, 26
Brentwood Farm Dairy, 54
Brighouse, Sam, 30, 34
Brighouse Racetrack, 30, 33, 34
Britannia Cannery, 23
Britannia Heritage Shipyards, 70, 72
Brooksband Dairy Farm, 54
brothels, 39
Brown's Dairy, 54
Brown, Roy, 54
Brownie, 44
Brunswick, SS, 8
Bryant, Alys McKey, 33
Burkeville, 48
bus service, 61

C

Canadian Northern Pacific Railway, 19, 20
Canadian Northern Railway, 19, 20
Canadian Pacific Railway, 2, 4, 5, 7, 8, 9, 12, 14, 19, 24, 44
canneries, 1, 4, 7, 8, 9, 21, 24, 39
Cedar Cottage, 27
Central Park Interurban, 11
Chahko Mika Mall, 68
Cheverton, Mrs. J., 63
Chevron, 58
Chilliwack, 52, 58
Chinatown, 38
City of Richmond, 22, 73
conductor, 14, 22, 40, 41, 42, 43, 44, 45, 48, 75
conductorettes, 48
Consolidated Railway and Light Corporation, 11
CPR, 2, 4, 5, 7, 8, 9, 12, 14, 19, 24, 44
CP Rail station, 23
CPR Sockeye Limited, 7

D

dairies, 54
dairy farmers, 51
dairy industry, 55
Deagle, Billie, 41
decommissioned, 61
depression, economic, 11
Diamond, Jack, 35
Dominion Day, 5

E

Eburne, 27
Eburne car, 12, 13
Eburne Post Office, 52
Electric Guides, 48
electricity, 55
Epsom Derby, 30
Ewen's Landing, 20
Ewen Cannery, 20

F

farmers, 22, 25, 51, 52
Father and Son Line, 48
final tram service, 61
First World War, 33
Fish, Amos, 54
fishing season, 8, 9, 39
Fogarty, Father Patrick, 41
Frasea Dairy Farm, 54
Fraser Valley, 52, 76
Fraser Valley Milk Producers' Association, 52

G

gambling houses, 39
Garden City Road, 14
Garry Point, 24, 25
gas rationing, 48
General Motors, 57, 58
George Star, SS, 8
Georghegan, Walter, 34
Golden Jubilee Handicap, 35
Governor General of Canada, 35
Granville Avenue, 14
Granville Depot, 29
Grauer, Jake, 54
Great Northern Railway, 20
Gulf of Georgia Cannery, 22

H

H.P. Dairy Farm, 54
Hall, Bert, 43, 65
Hall, Roy, 43
Hamilton, Charles K., 32
Hamre, Goodman, 58
Harper, Dolly, 40
Hastings Park, 34
Hewitt, James, 32
horse racing, 30
Horseshoe Bay, 58
hotels, 39
Hoy, Ernest C., 33

I

Imperial Cannery, 24
Indian Broom, 35
Inglewood township, 7
inspector, 45
interurban lines, 61

J

Jackson, John, 44
Johnson, E. Pauline, 38

K

Ken, Bill, 41
Kentucky Derby, 35
Kerrisdale, 14
King's Plate, 35
Kitsilano Bridge, 5
Kitsilano Trestle, 15

L

Ladner, 58
Lansdowne Park, 35
Lansdowne Racetrack, 34, 35, 37
Lion Island, 20
London Farm, 70
London Landing Development Corporation, 70
Lulu Island, 3, 2, 5, 6, 14, 3, 5, 7, 1, 2, 5, 6, 12, 25, 14, 22, 12, 14, 12, 21, 14, 19, 21, 19, 5, 19, 21, 6, 76, 19, 21, 76, 7, 5, 7, 15, 20, 25, 26, 32, 37, 38, 39, 42, 37, 38, 39, 42, 37, 38, 39, 42, 43, 44, 43, 44, 43, 44, 51, 54, 55, 51, 54, 55, 51, 54,

55, 61, 62, 61, 62, 61, 62, 73, 76, 22
Lulu Island line, 44, 61
Lulu Island Railway, 2, 6, 12

M

Magee Road, 7
Marpole, 5, 14, 15, 16, 22, 27, 28, 30, 35, 36, 41, 43, 48, 53, 76
Marpole/Eburne bridge, 16
Martin, Charlie, 41
McClelland, George, 52
McKay, D.E., 52
McLean, J.B., 52
McLennan, Al, 34
milk producers, 51
Minoru Park, 29, 32, 33, 37, 76
motorman, 14, 42, 43, 48
motormen, 41

N

Nelson Tramway Society, 68
New Westminster, 7, 8, 9, 11, 12, 15, 19, 22, 24, 27, 32
No.6 road, 22
No. 7 road, 22
Norgan, George, 34

O

Oak Street Bridge, 2
Oldfield, Charlie, 34
opium dens, 39
Orpheum, 37

P

Pacific Stage Lines, 57, 58
Pantages, 37
parachute jump, 33
Peanut Special, 38
Petty-Fitzmaurice, Henry Charles, 35
Pewitt, Clay, 35
Point Grey Municipality, 27
Portland streetcar system, 68

Port Mann, 19
Prestige Lakeside Resort and Conference Centre, 68
price of milk, 52

R

Racing Specials, 29
Rails to Rubbe, 58
Railway Avenue North, 14
Randall, Sam, 34
RAV line, 69
Richmond car, 12, 13
Richmond Heritage Railroad Society, 7, 67, 68, 69, 70, 71, 72, 76
Richmond Streetcar Feasibility Study, 69
ridership, 26, 61, 68
right rule, 15
Royal Mail, 1

S

salmon, 1, 8, 24, 39
saloons, 39
Sand Dunes, 24
Saunders, Charles, 33
Sea Island, 13, 42, 48
Second Narrows Bridge, 58
Shady Island, 24
Sharman, Vic, 7, 43, 45, 76
shipping
  hay, 25
  milk, 25, 51, 53
  oats, 25
Sloan Jr., Alfred P., 57
Sockeye Limited, 7, 8
Sockeye Special, 21, 37, 5, 6, 5, 6, 21, 72, 6, 72, 7, 3, 8, 19, 22, 32, 41, 7, 37, 41, 43, 44, 45, 48, 51, 67, 69, 72, 73, 72, 73, 72, 21
St. Anne's Anglican Church, 38
St. Anthony's Catholic Schoo, 41
St. Anthony of Padula Parish, 41
Stark, Billy M., 32

station, 26
  Alexandra, 15, 42
  Blundell, 15
  Branscomb, 15
  Branscombe, 26, 52
  Bridgeport, 15
  Brighouse, 15, 41
  Cambie, 15
  Davie Street, 40
  Eburne, 5, 7, 12, 13, 14, 15, 16, 24, 27, 30, 52, 76
  Garden City, 15
  Lulu, 15
  Magee, 5, 7
  Queensborough, 19
  Rifle Range, 15
  Sexsmith, 15, 52
  Steveston, 4, 5, 15, 19, 25
  Steveston Wye, 15
  Tucks, 15, 40
  Woodwards, 15
  Woodwards Landing, 19
sternwheeler, 8
Steve, Harold, 72
Steves, Billy, 1
Steves, Manoah, 52
Steveston car, 12, 13
Steveston Interurban Restoration Society, 67, 73, 75, 76
Steveston Opera House, 38
Steveston wharf, 24
streetcar, 61

T

tall ships, 24
Taylor, Austin, 35
Templeton, William, 32
Thompson, J, 51
time card, 45
Toonerville Trolley, 37
tram
  1205, 12
  1206, 12
  1207, 12, 61
  1208, 61
  1220, 67
  1222, 61
  1231, 61
tram crew, 23
trams, 14, 15, 17, 21, 29, 30, 37, 40, 43, 53, 61, 62, 77
Transfer, SS, 8
Translink, 70
Tuck, Mr., 17

U

University Dairy, 54
URS Engineering of Portland Oregon, 69

V

Vancouver, 7, 8, 1, 2, 4, 5, 7, 8, 9, 11, 12, 13, 14, 15, 19, 20, 21, 22, 26, 27, 30, 31, 32, 33, 34, 37, 38, 40, 41, 42, 44, 48, 49, 51, 52, 53, 57, 58, 59, 61, 71, 75, 76, 77
Vancouver & Lulu Island Railway, 2, 12
Vancouver depot, 15
Vancouver International Airport, 32

W

water tower, 20
West Coast Jockey Club Ltd., 34
Westermark, Dana, 70
Westminster and Vancouver Tramways Company, 11
whistle, 22, 62
White Star Motor Line, 58
Wilford Dairy, 54
women, 48
Woodwards Stores Ltd., 35
World War II, 48